SEA SHE
BRITISH A
EUROPEAN
COASTS

Josette Arrecgros

SPECTRUM
Colour Books

FOULIS

A SPECTRUM COLOUR BOOK

SEA SHELLS OF THE BRITISH AND EUROPEAN COASTS is published by
G T Foulis & Co Ltd of Sparkford, Yeovil, Somerset BA22 7JJ, England.
First published in German under the title **MUSCHELN AM MEER** by Hallwag AG of Bern, Switzerland

ISBN 0 85429 506 2

English language translation Elke and David Shackleton for "Accurate Translations", Maidenhead, Berkshire
Printed and bound by J H Haynes & Co Ltd Sparkford, Yeovil, Somerset
Cover photo Siegfried Eigstler

CONTENTS

A FEW BASIC IDEAS ABOUT SNAILS AND BIVALVES

Here we shall consider only the more common snails and bivalves. We shall not include rare species of molluscs which are of little concern to the 'non-scientific' collector.

Everyone knows the snail with its spitally coiled, calcareous shell. From the shell emerges a soft body whose ventral side forms a fleshy and muscular creeping foot. The calcareous shell is separated from the body by the skin, called the mantle.

Snails belong to the group of soft-bodied animals called molluscs.

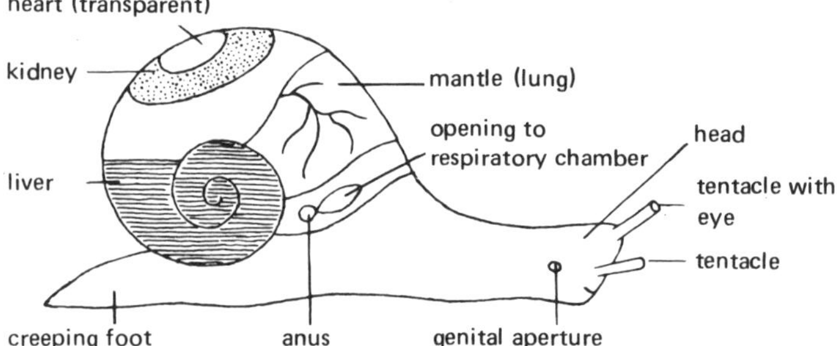

Land pulmonate snail without shell

Shell: in one piece.

Body: well-developed head; muscular creeping foot on the ventral side; lungs, or in the marine snails which belong to the same class, pinnate gills and an inhalant siphon which projects free in the water.

Snails belong to the gastropod class (Gastropoda = abdominal-footed).

The bivalve has a calcareous shell composed of two parts, the shell valves. If we examine a bivalve, we see that like the snail, it too has a soft body: it also belongs to the molluscs species. However, snails and bivalves exhibit very important differences which cause them to be separated into two classes: gastropods and lamellibranchs. The sketches on pages 4 and 5 make the differences clear.

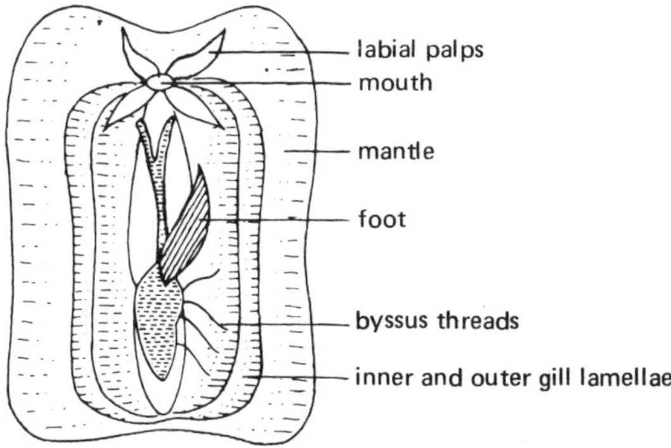

Bivalve without shell valves
(with mantle and gill lamellae spread out)

Shell: in two parts, shell valves.

Body: no proper head. Small, flattened, hatchet-shaped foot. Lamellar (plate-like) gills.

Bivalves belong to the lamellibranch class (lamella = plate, branchia = gills, plate-gilled).

An attempt at a classification of snails by the shell [1]

Model	Shell form	Family	Page
	Tube, more or less coiled	*Vermetidae*	12
opening	Flattened cone with opening at the apex	*Fissurellidae*	12
	Flattened cone without an opening	*Patellidae*	14
	Cone with slightly extened apex	*Capulidae*	14
	More or less spiral shell without an apex. Aperture extends down the whole length of the shell	*Cypraeidae*	16
		Marginellidae	16
		Scaphandridae	16
		Bullidae	16
	Ear-shaped shell, or shell with spiral whorls and a round aperture	*Haliotidae*	16
		Trochidae	18
		Turbinidae	20
		Eulimidae	22
		Scalidae	22
		Naticidae	22
		Truncatellidae	22
		Rissoidae	22
		Littorinidae	24
		Turritellidae	24
groove for inhalant siphon	Spirally coiled shell. Groove for the inhalant siphon at the aperture	*Apporrhaidae*	24
		Cerithiidae	24
		Doliidae	26
		Cassididae	26
		Tritonidae	26
		Muricidae	26
		Nassidae	28
		Columbellidae	30
		Buccinidae	30
		Fasciolariidae	30
		Mitridae	30
		Conidae	32
		Cancellariidae	32
		Turridae	32
		Acteonidae	32

[1] From *La Faune de la France*, by Remy-Perrier

An attempt at a classification of bivalves by the shell valves

Model	Valve form and adductor muscle scars in the shell valves	Family	Page
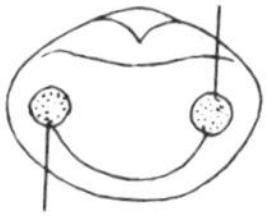 anterior adductor muscle posterior adductor muscle	Two similar adductor muscle scars, without a pallial sinus	*Nuculidae*	32
		Arcidae	34
		Isocardiidae	34
		Lucinidae	34
		Astartidae	36
		Chamidae	36
		Carditidae	36
		Cardiidae	36
 pallial sinus	Two similar or only slightly different adductor muscle scars, with a pallial sinus	*Veneridae*	38
		Petricolidae	40
		Donacidae	40
		Tellinidae	42
		Asaphidae	42
		Mactridae	44, 46
		Myidae	46, 48
		Saxicavidae	48
		Scrobiculariidae	48
		Thraciidae	48
		Pandoridae	48
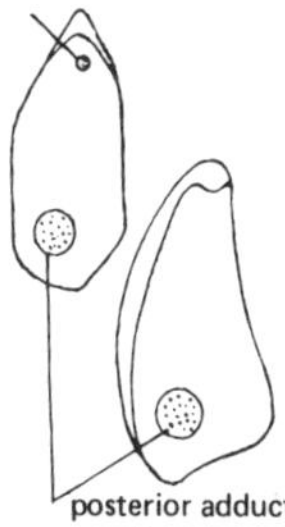 reduced anterior adductor muscle posterior adductor muscle	Two adductor muscle scars differing greatly in size, or only the scar of the anterior adductor muscle remaining	*Solenidae*	50
		Pholadidae	52
		Gastrochaenidae	52
		Teredinidae	52
		Pinnidae	52
		Pteriidae	54
		Mytilidae	54
		Pectinidae	56
		Spondylidae	58
		Limidae	58
		Ostreidae	58
		Anomiidae	58

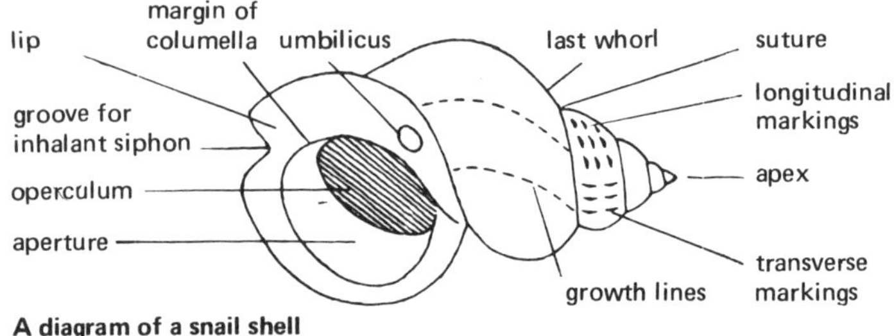

A diagram of a snail shell

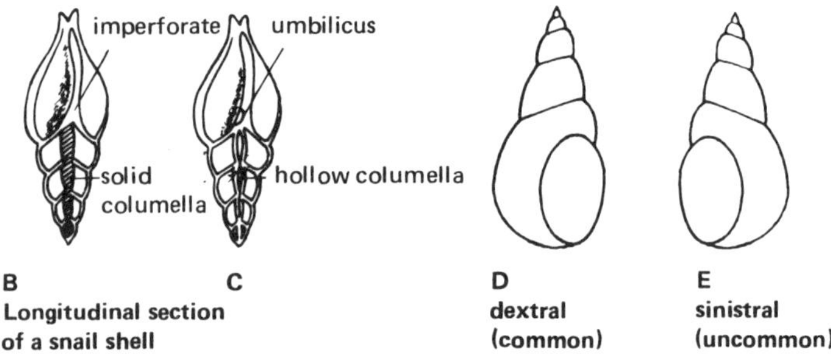

B **C**
Longitudinal section of a snail shell

D
dextral (common)

E
sinistral (uncommon)

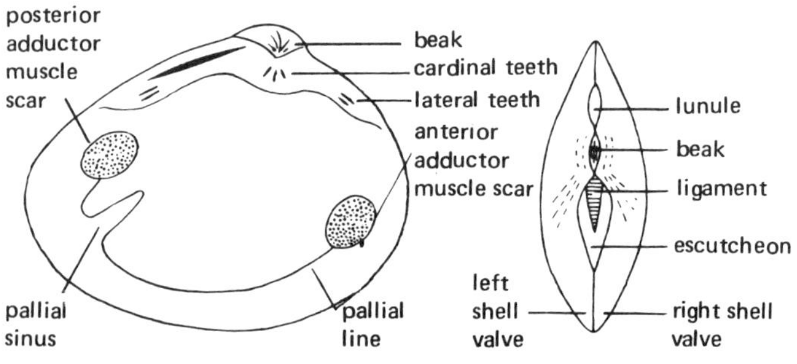

F bivalve: left shell valve, interior

G bivalve: shell valves, beak side

CHARACTERISTICS WE SHOULD NOTICE IN IDENTIFICATION

a) **Snail shells:**

1 Calcareous shell in one piece; in fresh condition, many specimens are covered by an epidermis *(periostracum)* (A).
2 Usually spirally coiled. Examine the shell with the apex pointing upwards, the aperture towards you. Aperture on the right side = dextral shell (common) (D). Aperture on the left side = sinistral shell (uncommon) (E).
3 The number of whorls varies. The apex is the first whorl; the last or youngest ends at the aperture, which is round or has a canal for the siphon.
4 The axis around which the whorls lie is called the columella: if it is hollow, the shell has an opening, the umbelicus, on the under side (C). If it is solid, the shell is termed imperforate (B). At the aperture the lip (curved outwards) and the columellar margin (curved inwards) can be distinguished.
5 The whorls of the spiral are separated by a groove, the suture.
6 Growth lines (gradual enlargement of the spiral) parallel to the lip.
7 Markings (ribs, bands, tubercles, etc.) run transversely and longitudinally.
8 The shell is sometimes closed by a calcareous or horny operculum.

b) **Bivalve shells:**

1 Calcareous shell, composed of two valves, right and left. They can be equivalve or inequivalve (F).
2 The apices of the valves are called beaks (G); the opening in front of the beak is the lunule, the one behind the beak is the escutcheon.
3 The part uniting the two valves is called the hinge; the ligament is situated either internally or externally.
4 Valve exterior: covered by a *periostracum*; growth lines running concentrically from the beak; markings (ribs, striae, etc.) concentric or radiating.
5 Valve interior: teeth: projections allowing the two valves to interlock; cardinal teeth below the beak, lateral teeth set a

little way back. The species is identified by the number and arrangement of the teeth. Scars of the soft animal body: anterior and posterior adductor muscles; pallial line, which often has an indentation (pallial sinus) if the animal possessed respiratory tubes (siphons).

6 To distinguish between the right and left valves: establish what is at the rear and what is at the front; a) when a pallial sinus is present; it is always posterior; b) if the ligament is on one side only, it is always posterior; c) if only one adductor muscle scar is observed, it is invariably the posterior one; d) the beak is often directed towards the front.

HINTS FOR THE PROSPECTIVE COLLECTOR

Where to find shells: At low tide in the most varied places, on the sand, on and amongst rocks, amongst algae, etc. Ask fishermen for molluscs which have been caught up in their nets or shrimp baskets. Look at the stalls in the fish market; the common edible molluscs are found there, but these may show characteristics peculiar to particular districts.

Preparation: If the animal is still in the shell, place it in boiling water for a few minutes, then carefully remove the body with tweezers; clean and dry the shell thoroughly (in the shade, as sunlight destroys the colours). Keep the operculum of snail shells, if present: plug the shell with cotton wool and paste the operculum onto the aperture.

Identifying the species: Use the coloured plates and the explanations opposite to them. A study of pages 4-9 will also make the task easier.

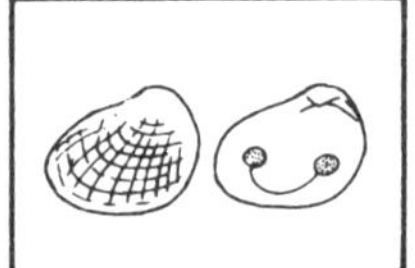

Arrangement of a pair of bivalve valves

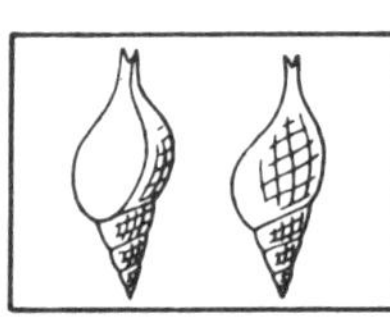

Arrangement of snail shells

Class: Gastropoda
Family: Muricidae
Murex brandaris L
Bordighera

Example of inscription

Storing the specimens: Keep small, fragile species in glass tubes, the others in different boxes. They can also be fixed to thick pieces of cardboard or glass plates, as follows:
bivalve shells:
left valve on the left
right valve on the right
beak at the top
pallial line at the bottom
one valve with the exterior displayed
one valve with the interior displayed
snail shells:
one example with the aperture displayed
one example with the whorls displayed
apex at the bottom
aperture at the top
Prepare a label for the glass plate or piece of cardboard showing in the sequence illustrated the class, family, Latin name, name of the naturalist who defined the species, English name and where it was found.

POSSIBLE USES

Various snail and bivalve shells can be used in the most attractive ways; the mother-of-pearl shells specially stir the imagination. For instance, the beautiful ormers with their artistic shape and mother-of-pearl interiors can be made into ashtrays. If the shell is attached to a pebble or a brightly coloured stone, the holes in the shell present no difficulties. Gapers and venus shells also make attractive ashtrays. First they should be cleaned, then they can be coated with a clear varnish so that they have a fresher effect. India-ink drawings on the inside give them a particularly attractive appearance. Necklaces and ear-rings made from small mother-of-pearl snail shells are sold at seaside resorts. These are top shells. The shells are first placed in hydrochloric acid, which removes the dull outer skin and allows the mother-of-pearl to be seen. They can also be prepared at home. A 10% solution of hydrochloric acid is used (dangerous, so handle with great care!), but be sure to place the water ready first and to pour the acid into it, never the other way round: the price of reversing the process could be one's eyesight! Almost as soon as the shells are placed in the solution, the mother-of-pearl appears. The process must be watched carefully so that the acid does not damage the mother-of-pearl as well. Afterwards, wash the shell in fast-running water, allow it to dry and gloss it with clear varnish. If a necklace is required, make a small hole in the edge of the aperture with a fine boring tool so that the shells can be strung. Thick bivalve shells can be used as salt-cellars if they are attached to a base, scallop shells serve as dishes for shellfish and hors-d'oeuvres. Artificial flowers can be made from the light mother-of-pearl shells of saddle oysters.

However, it should be left to the imagination of each individual to find new uses. The scope is limitless.

SNAILS

Worm Shells, *Vermetidae.* More or less irregular, tubular shell. Exclusively Mediterranean.

Not to be confused with the calcareous tubes of certain marine worms, the tube worms. Worm shells differ from the tubes of these worms in that the first loops are always spiral and the inner septa are convex; in addition, they are marked with longitudinal striae or they have scales on the inner surface.

1 *Vermetus triqueter.* Tube in more or less triangular segments, often with a raised dorsal line; 4-10 mm diameter. Adheres to stones or shells. Mediterranean. Common.

2 *Vermetus glomeratus* L. Small, spirally coiled, uniformly brown tube; 2-3 mm diameter. Lives free or adheres to shells. Mediterranean. Rather rare.

Slit Limpets and Keyhole Limpets, *Fissurellidae.* Conical shell, with a hole or longish slit at the apex.

3 *Fissurella reticulata* da Costa. Oval, shallow shell, 9-25 mm high; longitudinal ribs intersected by transverse ribs. Under stones. North Sea, Atlantic, Mediterranean. Fairly common.

4 *Emarginula elongata* O.G. Costa. Apex of the shell curved backwards; vertical slit at the back; 8-10 mm high. Mediterranean. Rather rare.

There are other species of Keyhole and Slit Limpets, but since they are very difficult to identify, we shall confine ourselves to these two.

1
4
8
2
9
3
5
7
6
11
10

Limpets, *Patellidae.* Shell shaped like a flat cone; apex imperforate; lacking calcareous plates on the inner surface.

5 **Common Limpet,** *Patella vulgata* L. Edible. Thick shell; apex almost in the centre; 30-40 mm diameter; 20-25 mm high; numerous irregular, radiating ribs. Adheres to stones. North Sea, Atlantic. Very common.

6 *Patella coerulea.* Edible. Generally the same form as above but thinner and very flat; finer radiating ribs; iridescent blue. Adheres to stones. Mediterranean. Very common.

7 *Patella intermedia (depressa).* Edible. Between examples five and six in height; radiating, protuberant ribs of orange and white. Adheres to stones. Atlantic (especially Bay of Biscay), very common. In the Mediterranean, Patella lusitanica with black spots.

8 **White Tortoiseshell Limpet,** *Acmaea virginea* Mull. Small, thin shell, whitish or pink; 10 mm high; apex not central. Under stones. North Sea, Atlantic. Common.

9 **Blue-rayed Limpet,** *Helcion pellucidus* L. Apex not central, very curved; 15-20 mm high; brown with fine blue striae. North Sea, Atlantic. Common.

Capulids, *Capulidae.* Shaped like the Cap of Liberty.

10 **Fools's Cap, Hungarian Cap, Cap of Liberty,** *Capulus hungaricus.* Shell covered by a yellow, velvety epidermis; 30-40 mm diameter. Attached to shells. North Sea, Atlantic, Mediterranean. Fairly common.

11 **American Slipper Limpet,** *Crepidula fornicata* L. Similar to No. 10, but differs in having a projecting calcareous ledge inside the aperture; 30-40 mm diameter. Adheres to mussel shells. North Sea, Atlantic. Rather rare.

12 *Crepidula anguiformis.* Very flat shell, calcareous ledge inside the aperture; 20-25 mm high. Mediterranean. Rather rare.

13 **Chinaman's Hat** or **Cup-and-saucer Limpet,** *Calyptrea chinensis L.* Apex in the centre very flattened; 20 mm diameter. Attached to bivalve shells. North Sea, Atlantic, Mediterranean. Common.

13

19

15

16

12

14

17

18

Cowries, *Cypraeidae.* More or less spiral without an apex; straight fissure down the whole length of the shell.

14 **Pear Cowrie,** *Cypraea pyrum.* Fawn-coloured, with brown, lustrous streaks; 40 mm long. Mediterranean. Rare.

15 **Lurid Cowrie,** *Cypraea lurida.* Duller than No. 14; 25-30 mm long. Mediterranean. Rare.

16 **European Cowry,** *Trivia europaea* Mtg. Only 8-12 mm long, greyish-pink, often with brown spots; finely striated; aperture very notched. North Sea, Atlantic, Mediterranean. Fairly common.

17 *Pseudosinarica adriatica.* Thin, whitish, egg-shaped shell; 20-25 mm. Mediterranean. Rare.

18 *Pseudosinarica carnea.* Smaller than No. 17, 10-15 mm; pale pink. Mediterranean. Rare.

Marginellids, *Marginellidae.* Conical shells.

19 *Marginelia milaria.* Shell shaped like a millet seed; 7 mm long. Mediterranean. Fairly common.

Scaphandrids, *Scaphandridae.* Shell partially covered by the mantle lobes of the animal's body.

20 **Canoe Shell,** *Scaphander lignarius* L. Shell in the form of a yellowish-brown horn. Height 70 mm. Atlantic, Mediterranean. Fairly common.

Bubble shells, *Bullidae.* As in the scaphandrids the shell is partly concealed by the mantle lobes.

21 **Striale Bubble,** *Bulla striata.* Same shape as the canoe shell, but only 20-30 mm high; mottled grey with darker spots. Mediterranean. Rare.

22 *Haminea navicula (Bulla hydatis).* Thin, fragile shell; 25 mm high; light brown; aperture extends forwards. North Sea, Atlantic, Mediterranean. Rare.

Ormers, *Haliotidae.* Shell spiral, ear-shaped, interior mother-of-pearl.

23 **Ormer** or **Sea Ear,** *Haliotis tuberculata* L. Edible. Mother-of-pearl shell 60-80 mm in size; a row of holes along the left-hand margin (5-6, those at the rear vestigial); brown and greenish-red periostracum; more or less tubercular small plates on the outside; interior lined thickly with

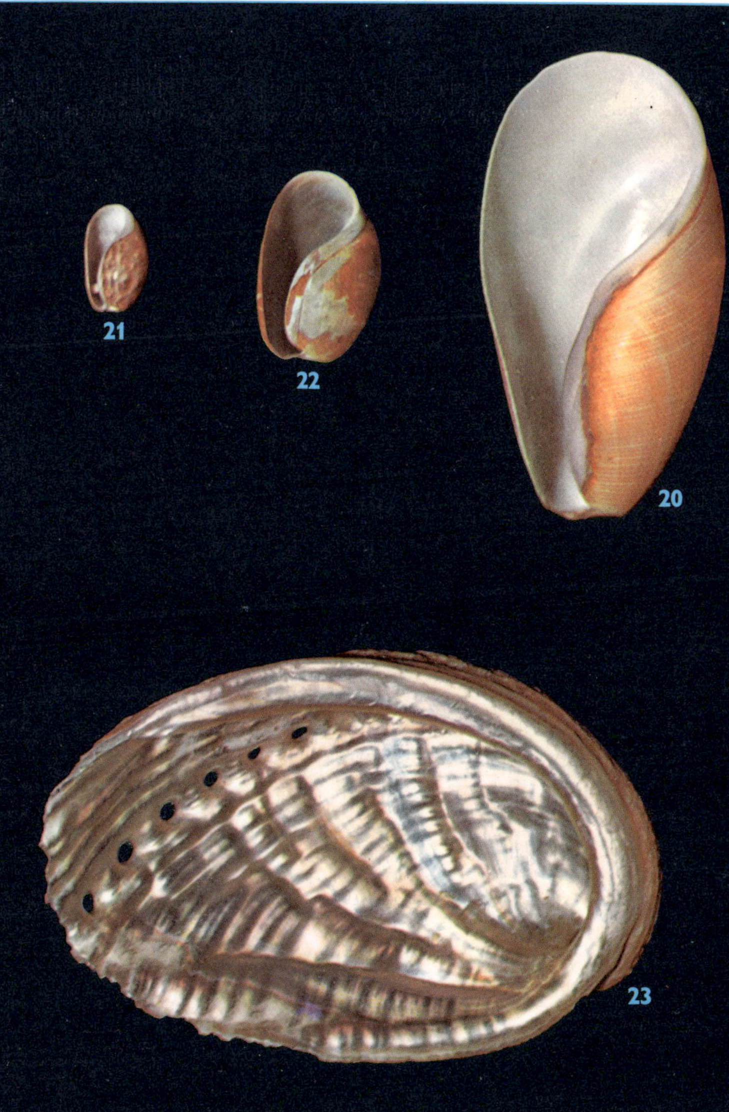
21
22
20
23

mother-of-pearl, beautifully iridescent. Adheres to undersides of stones. North Sea, Atlantic. Fairly common. In the Mediterranean, a smaller species with more distinct plates.

Next plate page 19:

Top Shells, *Trochidae.* Spiral shell with a round, often mother-of-pearl aperture.

24 **Thick top,** *Monodonta lineata* da Costa. Bulky, grey, striated with dark, oblique markings; imperforate; 15-25 mm diameter. Lives on rocks. North Sea, Atlantic. Very common.

25 *Monodonta turbinata.* Similar in form to No. 24, but with more distinct violet spots; 20-25 mm diameter. On rocks. Mediterranean. Very common.

26 *Monodonta articulata.* Shape of shell as in Nos. 24 and 25, but marked with clearly separated red spots; 20 mm diameter. On rocks. Mediterranean. Common.

27 *Gibbula magus.* Tubercles on the whorls; umbelicus; distinctive colouring with red streaks, 20-30 mm diameter. Lives in sand. North Sea, Atlantic, Mediterranean. Common.

28 *Gibbula divaricata.* Small, scattered red spots on a greenish background; umbilicus reduced or not present; 15-18 mm diameter. Mediterranean. Very common.

29 *Gibbula richardi.* Orange dots, especially underneath; last whorl very large; 15-20 mm diameter. Mediterranean. Common.

30 *Gibbula varia.* Shape variable; often obliquely streaked with grey; 10-15 mm diameter. Mediterranean. Very common.

31 **Flat Top** or **Purple Top,** *Gibbula umbilicalis* da Costa. Streaked with violet, streaks distinct, broad and widely spaced; aperture oblique; 15-20 mm diameter. North Sea, Atlantic. Very common.

32 **Grey Top** or **Silver Tommy,** *Gibbula cineraria* L. Similar to those above, but with a taller spire; finely striated with black, oblique markings. North Sea, Atlantic. Common.

33 *Gibbula adansoni.* Small shell, taller than it is broad; brown with small white streaks; 10 mm diameter. Mediterranean.

24
25
26
28
27
29
33
32
30
31
36
37
34
35
38
39
40

Common.

34 **Painted Top,** *Calliostoma zizyphinum* L. Large, top-shaped, pointed shell with nongranulated longitudinal striae and bright-red spots; 25-30 mm diameter. North Sea, Atlantic, Mediterranean. Very common.

35 *Calliostoma granulata.* Very similar to No. 34, but with finer striae, and granulated; 30 mm diameter. North Sea, Atlantic, Mediterranean. Common.

36 **Jujube Top Shell,** *Jujubinus exasperatus (Calliostoma jujubinum).* Very small, a vivid red, with very finely granulated striae; 5-7 mm diameter. North Sea, Atlantic, Mediterranean. Very common.

37 **Striated Top,** *Jujubinus striatus* L. Small shell with slightly convex whorls and fine, smooth, longitudinal stripes; 8-10 mm diameter. North Sea, Atlantic, Mediterranean. Rather rare.

38 *Clanculus corallinus.* Small, coral-red shell with double dentation at the base of the columella; 10 mm diameter. Mediterranean. Rather rare.

39 *Clanculus cruciatus.* Similar to No. 38, but with simple dentation at the base of the columella; rust-brown, sometimes streaked with white; 10 mm diameter. Mediterranean. Rather rare.

40 *Clanculus Jussieui.* Similar to Nos. 38 and 39, but with fine, grey, oblique streaks spaced at regular intervals; 14 mm diameter. Mediterranean. Rather rare.

Turbinids, *Turbinidae.* Shell spiral, with round aperture.

41 *Astraea rugosa.* Thick shell with tubercles or spines; 30-40 mm diameter. Bay of Biscay, Mediterranean. Rather rare.

42 *Homalopoma sanguinea.* Small, bright red, height and width the same; broad longitudinal ribs; 8 mm diameter. Mediterranean. Rather rare.

43a **Pheasant Shell,** *Phasianella pullus* L. Small, with pointed spire, brown spots on a pink background; 5-8 mm. Under algae. North Sea, Atlantic. Very common.

43b An even more pointed variation. Mediterranean.

42
43 a
43 b
41
46
44
45
47
48
51
49
50
52

Eulimids, *Eulimidae.* Small, smooth, with a long coiled spire, pointed.

44 *Eulima subulata.* Pale-yellow shell, often with darker spots; 7-8 mm. Mediterranean. Rather rare.

45 *Eulima incurva.* Very small, curved shell, white; 2-3 mm. North Sea, Atlantic, Mediterranean. Rather rare.

Wentletraps or **Staircase Shells,** *Scalidae.* Turretted shells, with many whorls and a round aperture; umbilicate.

46 **Common Wentletrap,** *Scala clathrus* L. Pale violet with broad, regularly spaced, oblique ribs; 3 cm high. North Sea, Atlantic, Mediterranean. Common.

Necklace Shells, *Naticidae.* Globose, polished shells with few whorls and a broad umbelicus.

47 *Natica millepunctata.* Has dense, dark-brown dots; a thin buttress projects down into the umbelicus; 3-4 mm diameter. Mediterranean. Fairly common.

48 *Natica hebraea.* Very similar to No. 47, but with irregular patches instead of dots. Mediterranean. Fairly common.

49 **Large Necklace Shell,** *Lunatia catena* da Costa. Globose, with a band of brown patches round each whorl; 30-40 mm diameter. No buttress in the umbelicus. North Sea, Atlantic, Mediterranean. Common.

50 *Neverita josephina.* Very flat shell; umbelicus containing a very convoluted buttress; yellowish-grey tone; 35 mm diameter. Mediterranean. Fairly common.

51 *Lunatia poliani.* Small shell, 15 mm in diameter; rust-red streaks; umbelicus half concealed by the inner lip. Atlantic, Mediterranean. Fairly common.

52 *Payraudautia intricata.* Very similar to No. 51, but umbelicus has two spiral ridges. Mediterranean. Fairly common.

Truncatellids, *Truncatellidae.* Truncated spiral.

53 *Truncatella laevigata.* Smooth, pale yellow; 5-6 mm tall. North Sea, Atlantic, Mediterranean. Rather rare.

Spire shells, *Rissoidae.* Small shells with round aperture; imperforate. Numerous species, but difficult to distinguish.

54
55
56 a
57
53
56 b
58
56 c
59
61 b
61 a
64
65
60 a
60 b
63
62

54 *Rissoa membranacea.* 6 mm; violet aperture, transverse striae. Atlantic. Very common.

55 *Rissoa cimex.* Pale yellow, finely striated; 6-8 mm high. Mediterranean. Common.

Winkles or **Periwinkles,** *Littorinidae.* Small spire, few whorls and a round aperture.

56a, b,c **Flat Winkle,** *Littorina obtusata* L. Blunt shell, the last whorls globose; colouring varied. On algae. Atlantic. Common.

57 **Common Winkle,** *Littorina littorea* L. Edible. Regular spire. On rocks. Atlantic.

58 **Rough Winkle,** *Littorina saxatilis* Olivi. Similar to No. 57. Spire less regular, 15 mm. On rocks. Atlantic. Common.

59 **Small Winkle,** *Littorina neritoides* L. Very small species, 5-8 mm; blue-black. Bay of Biscay, Mediterranean. Very common.

Screw Shells, *Turritellidae.* Tall, spiral shells, pointed and turretted, with many whorls and a round aperture.

60a **Screw Shell, Auger** or **Tower Shell,** *Turritella communis* Risso. Longitudinal striae; 40-60 mm; whorls convex. North Sea, Atlantic, Mediterranean. Common.

60b Variation, whorls not convex.

Pelican's Foot Shells, *Apporrhaidae.* Lip expanded to form finger-like processes (digitations).

61a **Pelican's Foot Shell,** *Apporrhais pes-pelicani* L. 30-40 mm; lip has three digitations; whorls tuberculated. Atlantic, Mediterranean. Common.

61b Mediterranean variation with longer digitations.

Needle Whelks, *Cerithiidae.* Tall, spiral shells with many whorls and a short, twisted siphonal canal.

62 *Cerithium vulgatum.* Large shell, height of spire 40-60 mm, last whorl somewhat broader than the rest, small tubercles. On rocks. Common in the Mediterranean, rare in the Atlantic.

63 *Cerithium rupestre.* Smaller than No. 62 (25 mm). Idem.

68
66
67
70
71
72
73
74

64 **Small Needle Whelk,** *Bittium reticulatum* da Costa. 10-13 mm; four rows of tubercles. North Sea, Atlantic, Mediterranean. Very common.

65 *Triforis perversa.* Very similar to No. 64, but sinistral. North Sea, Atlantic, Mediterranean. Rather rare.

Doliids, *Doliidae.* Large, globose, thin shells.

66 **Giant Tun, Helmet Tun or Spotted Tun,** *Tonna galea (Dolium galea).* Large, 100-150 mm, with regular spiralling grooves. Mediterranean. Rare.

Cassidids, *Cassididae.* Large, ventricose shells, thicker than in the doliids.

67 *Cassis saburon.* Attractive shell, 50-70 mm tall, finely scored with regular, smooth, longitudinal markings. Bay of Biscay, Mediterranean. Fairly common. Similar species, *Cassis undulata Gm.,* more sparsely striated.

68 *Galeodea echinophora.* Large, 50-60 mm high, shaped like No. 67, but the aperture lacks folds; broad margin of the columellar lip turned outwards; longer siphonal canal; large tubercles arranged in rows. Mediterranean. Fairly common. G. tyrrhena Ch. has longitudinal, untuberculated ribs.

Tritonids, *Tritonidae.* Very large, horn-shaped shells.

69 *Tritonalia nodifer.* Can measure up to 300 mm; tuberculate; yellowish with brown spots; aperture white, with crenated lip spotted brown; short siphonal canal. Atlantic, Mediterranean. Fairly common. (Illustration on front cover).

70 *Cyonatium (cymatium) corrigatum.* 60-90 mm high, covered with a velvety periostracum. Mediterranean. Fairly common.

71 *Cyonatium cutaceum.* 50-80 mm tall, with parchment-like periostracum. Mediterranean. Fairly common.

72 *Ranella gigantea (olearium).* 50-180 mm high, with tuberculated spire (traces of the aperture lip, therefore shell was still growing). Mediterranean. Rather rare.

Whelks, *Muricidae.* Thick, tuberculated shells, siphonal canal in anterior right-hand region.

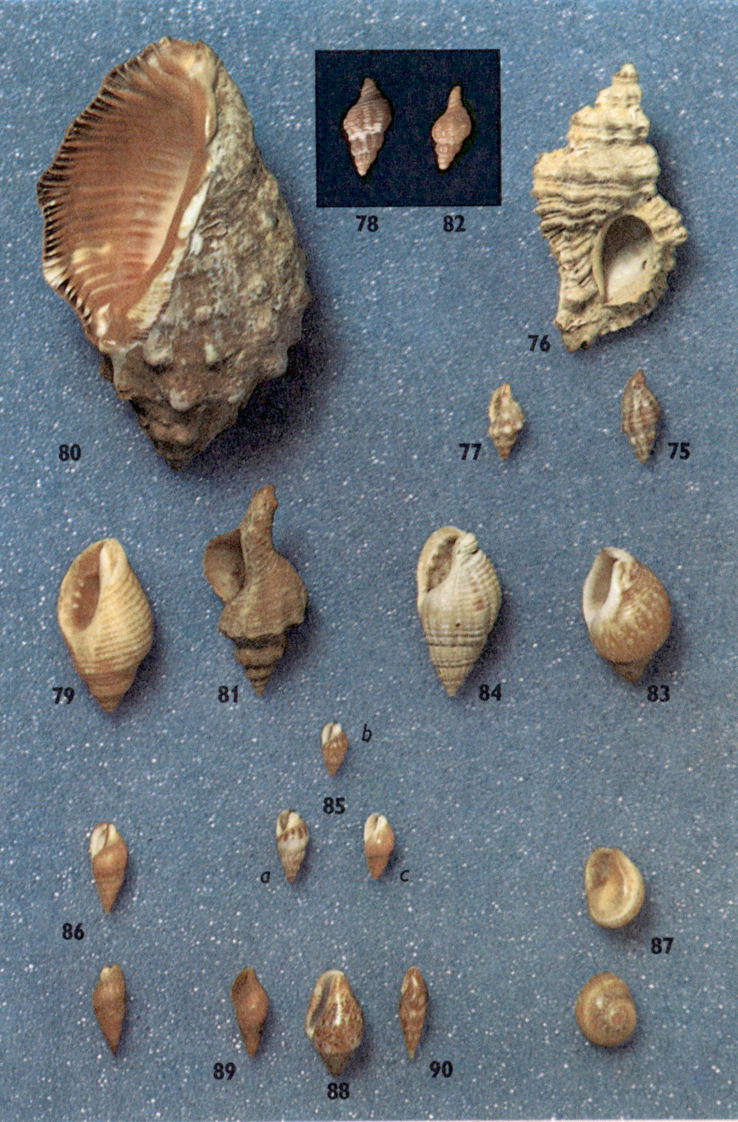
78
82
76
80
77
75
79
81
84
83
b
85
a
c
86
87
89
88
90

73 **Spiny Dye Murex,** *Murex brandaris.* Edible. Ventricose shell, 50-80 mm; siphonal canal longer than the aperture, large spines. Mediterranean. Common.

74 **Banded Dye Murex,** *Murex trunculus*. Edible. Ventricose shell, 50-80 mm; grey, with brown bands; canal shorter than the aperture; shorter spines than in No. 73. Mediterranean. Common. In classical times the mollusc inhabiting the shell was used as a purple fabric dye and was an important trading commodity.

75 *Muricopsis blainvillei.* 10-25 mm; short canal; distinct striae and narrow spines. On rocks. Mediterranean. Common.

76 **Sting Winkle** or **Drill,** *Ocenebra erinacea* L. Feeds on other molluscs by boring through the shells, Shell is 30-40 mm, thick, rugose, with ridges, siphonal canal short. North Sea, Atlantic, Mediterranean. Fairly common.

77 *Ocenebra edwardsi.* 10-18 mm; often has two brown bands encircling each whorl. Basque coast, Mediterranean. Fairly common.

78 *Ocenebra corallina.* Very similar to No. 77, but smaller (6-8 mm), intense brown. North Sea, Atlantic. Common.

79 **Dog Whelk,** *Purpura lapillus* L. 20-25 mm high, often with black or yellow bands. Thick, dentate aperture. On coastal rocks. North Sea, Atlantic. Very common.

80 *Purpura haemastoma* Z. 40-80 mm; orange aperture. Mediterranean, Basque coast. Rather rare.

81 *Hadriania craticulata.* 2-4 cm; siphonal canal closed; decussated by ribs. Mediterranean. Rather rare.

82 *Trophon muricatus.* 6-8 mm; longitudinal striae and transverse ridges. North Sea, Atlantic, Mediterranean. Rather rare.

Dog Whelks, *Nassidae.* Very varied shells.

83 *Nassa mutabilis.* Swollen shell, 25-30 mm high; mottled white and brown. Mediterranean. Fairly common.

84 **Netted Dog Whelk,** *Nassa reticulata* L. 20-30 mm; decussated by ridges. North Sea, Atlantic, Mediterranean. Very common.

85a **Thick-lipped Dog Whelk,** *Nassa incrassata* Muller. As No. 84, but much smaller (10-12 mm); thickened lip. Atlantic,

91
92
93
96
95
94
97
100
101
99
98
102

North Sea, Mediterranean.

85b,c *Nassa pygmea.* Dwarfish variation.

86 *Nassa corniculum.* Shape as in Nos. 84 and 85, but with smooth sculpturing; 18-20 mm; punctuate longitudinal band. On rocks. Fairly common in Bay of Biscay. Very common in Mediterranean.

87 *Cyclope neritea.* Round shell, flat at the base; orange streaks. Basque coast, Mediterranean. Common.

Columbellids, *Columbellidae.* Large aperture (more than 2/3 of the height of the shell). Mediterranean.

88 *Columbella rustica (Pyrene rustica).* 15-18 mm; very long aperture; whitish, streaked with orange. On rocks.

89 *Columbella gervillei.* More oblong than No. 88; 20 mm; light brown. Rather rare.

90 *Columbella scripta.* 15-20 mm high; whitish, with irregular orange markings. Rather rare.

Whelks and **Buckies,** *Buccinidae.* Pointed, spiralled shells, the short siphonal canal twisted back sharply.

91 **Whelk** or **Common Whelk,** *Buccinum undatum* L. Strong, solid shell; 60-70 mm; large, oblique, undulating corrugations. Atlantic. Fairly common.

92 *Euthria cornea.* Smooth; 40-50 mm; light brown, with dark streaks; thin ridge along the suture between the whorls. Mediterranean. Rather rare. In the Atlantic, Colus Jeffreysianus, variation without the ridge. Rare.

93 *Pisania maculosa.* 20-25 mm; olive green and brown, with black dots in regular rows; aperture violet, crenated. On rocks. Mediterranean. Common. P. orbinia Payr has longitudinal folds and transverse striae.

Spindle Shells, *Fasciolariidae.* Spindle-shaped shells.

94 *Fusus (Frisinus) rostratus.* 40-50 mm, with a long siphonal canal. Mediterranean. Fairly common.

Mitrids, *Mitridae.* Narrow spire, columella folded.

95 *Mitra ebenus.* Dark brown, with a light band; spire 18 mm high. Mediterranean. Fairly common.

107
108
109
110
111
105
106
112
104
103

96 *Mitra cornicula.* Narrower than No. 95; light brown. Mediterranean. Fairly common.

97 *Mitra tricolor.* Smaller than Nos. 95 and 96 (8-10 mm); white, yellow and brown bands. Mediterranean. Fairly common.

Conids, *Conidae.* Conical shells.

98 **Mediterranean Cone,** *Conus mediterraneus.* 30 mm.

Cancellariids, *Cancellariidae.* One species only.

99 *Cancellaria cancellata.* Attractive shell, 35 mm high, with spiralling brown bands. Mediterranean. Rather rare.

Turrids, *Turridae.* Small, turret-shaped shells.

100 *Mangilia purpurea.* 8-20 mm; brown and violet; decussated. Atlantic, Mediterranean. Fairly common.

101 *Mangilia Vauquelini.* Whitish, with prominent ribs. Mediterranean. Rare.

Acteon Shells, *Acteonidae.* In the living animal, the shell is partially covered by the mantle lobes.

102 **Acteon Shell** or **Beer Barrel,** *Acteon tornatilis* L. Grey and pink, with three thin white bands; height of spire 25 mm. Rather rare in the North Sea. More common in Bay of Biscay, Mediterranean.

BIVALVES

Nut Shells, *Nuculidae.* Adductor muscle scars equal; no pallial sinus; row of teeth resembling a comb broken in the middle.

103 *Nucula nucleus.* Small shells 10 mm in length, a minute oval in shape, mother-of-pearl interior. Exterior smooth, lightly scored with concentric lines. North Sea, Atlantic, Mediterranean. Fairly common.

104 *Nucula sulcata.* Very similar to No. 103, but with distinct concentric striae. North Sea, Atlantic, Mediterranean. Rather rare.

105 *Nuculana fragilis.* Small, 8 mm long, pointed at the back. Atlantic, Mediterranean. Rather rare.

106 *Nuculana pella.* Very similar to No. 105, but somewhat larger, 9-15 mm long; posterior notch. Mediterranean. Rare.

113

Ark Shells and **Dog Cockles,** *Arcidae.* Equal adductor muscle scars; no pallial sinus; teeth in a straight line, as in a comb.

107 **Dog Cockle** or **Comb Shell,** *Glycymeris* glycymeris L. Edible. Thick, round, large shell, 40-60 mm in diameter, with velvet-like periostracum; white with brown markings. North Sea, Atlantic, Mediterranean. Common.

108 *Glycymeris violascens.* Very similar to No. 107, but larger. Mediterranean. Common.

109 **Bearded Ark Shell,** *Arca barbata (Barbatia barbata).* Inequilateral, solid, with more or less numerous ribs; roughly boat-shaped; 20-50 mm long; periostracum with long, coarse, blackish hairs. Mediterranean. Fairly common.

110 **Noah's Ark Shell,** *Arca Noae* L. Similar to No. 109, but thicker; prominent ribs; light brown; 50-80 mm. North Sea, Atlantic, Mediterranean. Common.

111 **Ark Shell,** *Arca tetragona* Poli. Thinner shells than in No. 110, posterior flatter; 20-35 mm long. Atlantic, Mediterranean. Common.

112 **Milky Ark Shell,** *Arca lactea* L. A small version, the same shape as No. 111, 14 mm long; milk white, covered with a velvety periostracum. North Sea, Atlantic, Mediterranean. Very common.

Heart Cockles, *Isocardiidae.* Adductor muscle scars equal; no pallial sinus; large, regular valves.

113 **Heart Cockle,** *Isocardia cor* L. Solid shell 60-120 mm in diameter, with markedly enrolled beaks. Atlantic, Mediterranean. Fairly common.

Next plate:

Lucines or **Hatchet Shells,** *Lucinidae.* Adductor muscle scars equal; no pallial sinus; teeth under the beak wide apart; thin, round shells.

114 *Myrtea spinifera (Lucina spinifera).* Thin shells, concentric ridges with spiny edges; 12 mm long, 9 mm high. North Sea, Atlantic, Mediterranean. Rare.

115 *Loripes lactus.* Round, milk-white shells; 15-25 mm diameter; adductor muscle scars very unequal. Atlantic,

114
115
116
117
122 a
123
118
122 b
121
124
119
120

Mediterranean. Very common.

116 **Round Double-tooth,** *Diplodonta rotundata.* Very similar to No. 115, but differs in having a more yellow colouring and more equal adductor muscle scars. North Sea, Atlantic, Mediterranean. Fairly common.

Astartes, *Astartidae.* Adductor muscle scars equal; no pallial sinus; concentrically striated.

117 *Astarte fusca.* Shells 20 mm in diameter, brown, with prominent concentric ridges. Mediterranean. Rather rare.

Chamids, *Chamidae.* Adductor muscle scars equal; no pallial sinus; valves of unequal thickness.

118 *Chama gryphoides.* 15-20 mm diameter; very irregular valves, covered in small scales which form concentric rows. Mediterranean. Rather rare.

Carditids, *Carditidae.* Adductor muscle scars equal; no pallial sinus; thick-set, almost square shells; 2 wide-spaced teeth below the beak, lateral teeth sometimes present.

119 *Venericardia sulcata.* 20-30 mm diameter; 12-20 broad, radiating ribs with concentric striae; outer surface dark brown. Mediterranean. Common.

120 *Cardita calyculata.* Square shell; 20 mm long; thick, with scaly ribs. Lives in crevices of rocks, and therefore deformed. Mediterranean. Fairly common.

121 *Cardita trapezia.* Almost as broad as long, with scaly ribs; 8-9 mm broad. Mediterranean. Rather rare.

Cockles, *Cardiidae.* Adductor muscle scars equal; no pallial sinus; equilateral, with lateral teeth.

122a **Prickly Cockle,** *Cardium echinatum* L. Edible. Thick; 40-50 mm long; 25-30 short-spined ribs separated by grooves. North Sea, Atlantic, Mediterranean. Fairly common. Also in the North Sea, Atlantic and Mediterranean is found the related species:

122b *Cardium paucicostatum.* Smaller than No. 122a, with fewer ribs.

123 **Spiny Cockle,** *Cardium aculeatum* L. Edible. 35-80 mm diameter; ribs with hook-shaped spines. Mediterranean. Common.

126
127
128
125

124 **Common** or **Edible Cockle,** *Cardium edule* L. Small shell 25-45 mm in diameter; 24-26 flat, scaly ribs. North Sea, Atlantic, Mediterranean. Very common.

125 **Spiny Cockle,** *Cardium tuberculatum (Acanthocardia tuberculata).* Edible. Thick shell, length 40-60 mm; strong, tuberculated ribs. Atlantic, Mediterranean. Common.

126 *Cardium norvegicum (Laevicardium crassum).* Thick, 30-60 mm long; slightly protruding ribs which die out towards the beak. North Sea, Atlantic, Mediterranean. Common.

127 *Cardium oblongum.* Very similar to No. 126, but rather more elongated. Mediterranean. Fairly common.

Venus Shells or **Venus Clams,** and **Carpet Shells,** *Veneridae.* Adductor muscle scars equal; pallial sinus; regular shape with 3 wide-spaced teeth below the beak.

128 **Warty Venus,** *Venus verrucosa* L. Edible. Large shell, 30-50 mm long; covered by irregular, concentric laminae with wart-like tubercles. Colour rusty orange. North Sea, Atlantic, Mediterranean. Common. A second, similar species, *Venus casina* L., with concentric, untuberculated laminae, lives in the Mediterranean.

129 **Striped Venus,** *Venus gallina (striatula).* Edible. 30-35 mm long; irregular ribs running concentrically in pairs; whitish, with 3 orange rays. Rather rare in Atlantic. Common in Mediterranean.

130 **Banded Venus,** *Venus fasciata.* 13-25 mm long; covered with flat, concentric laminae; orange, with radiating bands of brown, more or less faded. North Sea, Atlantic. Rather rare.

131 **Oval Venus,** *Venus ovata.* Small, 9-12 mm long; decussated; whitish colour. North Sea, Atlantic, Mediterranean. Very common.

132 **Rayed Artemis,** *Dosinia exoleta* L. Edible. 20-40 mm long, with strong growth lines; white, often with brown bands. North Sea, Atlantic, Mediterranean. Common. In the Atlantic and especially in the Mediterranean, a similar species, the **Smooth Artemis,** *Dosinia lupinus* L.; smaller, yellow and white.

129
132
131
130
133
134 a
134 b

133 *Macrocallista chione.* Edible. 50-70 mm long; smooth, pale periostracum; sometimes with more or less distinct radiating striae. Atlantic, Mediterranean. Common.

134a **Cross-cut Carpet Shell,** *Venerupis decussatus* L. Edible. Shells 20-60 mm long, decussated; fawn, with 3 rays of brown spots. Mediterranean. Very common.

134b In the Atlantic there is a lighter-coloured variation, **Cross-cut Carpet Shell,** *Venerupis decussata var. fuscus.*

135a **Golden Carpet Shell,** *Venerupis aureus* Gm. Edible. Small species, 17-25 mm in diameter; a distinctive feature is the gold and yellow colouring on the inside; on the outside, brown, hieroglyphic-style markings. North Sea, Atlantic, Mediterranean. Common.

135b A Mediterranean variation, *Venerupis texturatus.*, has more prominent sculpturing.

136 **Banded Carpet Shell,** *Venerupis rhomboideus* Penn. 20-50 mm long; concentric striae; colours very varied. North Sea, Atlantic, Mediterranean. Common.

137a **Pullet Carpet Shell,** *Venerupis pullastra* Wood. 15-18 mm long; decussated, but concentric striae more prominent than in 134a. North Sea, Atlantic, Mediterranean. Common.

137b A Mediterranean variation, *Venerupis geographicus,* is rather smaller and more oblong.

138 *Irus irus.* Shape very variable; 20-25 mm long; covered with scaly, overlapping laminae. Lives in rock crevices. North Sea, Atlantic, Mediterranean. Fairly common.

Petricolids, *Petricolidae.* Adductor muscle scars equal; pallial sinus; thin, brittle shells; 2 teeth below the beak; short anterior region.

139 *Petricola lithophaga.* Rounded at the front, blunt-cornered at the back; 10-30 mm long. Lives in rocks. North Sea, Atlantic, Mediterranean. Rather rare.

Wedge Shells, *Donacidae.* Adductor muscle scars equal; pallial sinus; polished shells; anterior region shorter than posterior.

140 *Donax politus.* Edible. 20-40 mm long; white tinged with violet, sometimes yellowish with darker bands; interior violet, inner margin notched. North Sea, Atlantic,

135 a
135 b
137 a
136
137 b
138
139
141
140

Mediterranean. Very common.

141 *Donax semistriatus.* Edible. More oblong than No. 140; transversely striated as far as the centre of the shell. Mediterranean. Fairly common.

Tellins, *Tellinidae.* Adductor muscle scars equal; pallial sinus; thin, brittle shells; similar in shape to wedge shells, but the inner margin is never notched.

142 **Blunt Tellin,** *Arcopagia crassa* L. Thick, round shell, 23-40 mm long; white, sometimes with pink rays. Atlantic. Fairly common.

143a *Angulus planatus.* Oblong shell, 30-40 mm long; interior tinged with pink. Mediterranean. Rather rare.

143b *Angulus nitidus.* Similar in form to No. 143a, but smaller; interior yellow and orange. Also inhabits the Mediterranean, but is rare.

144 *Angulus incarnatus.* Flesh-coloured, very brittle, inequilateral; 15-30 mm long. Atlantic, Mediterranean. Rather rare.

145 **Thin Tellin,** *Angulus tenuis* da Costa. Small, very thin shells of variable colouring, white, yellow or pink. After the animal dies, the valves gape like butterfly wings. North Sea, Atlantic, Mediterranean. Very common.

146 *Gastrana fragilis.* 18-30 mm long, brittle; small, densely-spaced ribs and laminated, concentric striae; colour yellowish white. Atlantic, Mediterranean, in brackish waters. Fairly common.

Sunset Shells, *Asaphidae.*

147 **Large Sunset Shell,** *Psammobia depressa (Gari depressa).* 40-60 mm long; pink and grey, often with pink rays; parchment-like periostracum at the edges. North Sea, Atlantic, Mediterranean. Common.

148 **Faroe Sunset Shell,** *Psammobia feroensis (Gari ferrensis).* 10-35 mm long, oblong, truncated posteriorly; violet and white, often with yellow and red rays. North Sea, Atlantic, Mediterranean. Rather rare.

142
143 a
144
143 b
145
146
148
147

Trough and **Otter Shells,** *Mactridae.* Adductor muscle scars equal; pallial sinus; ligament internal, in a triangular pit (chondrophore) behind the cardinal teeth.

149 *Mesodesma corneum.* Small shell, 15-20 mm long; form as in wedge shells, but with the characteristic hinge of the trough shells. North Sea, Atlantic, Mediterranean. Fairly common.

150 **Rayed Trough Shell,** *Mactra corallina* L. Edible. Globose shell, 40-50 mm in diameter; yellowish rays on a violet background; the dirty-grey periostracum often clings persistently to the shell. Two variations: a) stultorum, in the Mediterranean; b) atlantica, somewhat rounder and duller, in the Atlantic. Both common.

151 *Mactra glauca.* Edible. Less ventricose than No. 150; 40-100 mm long, with yellow, velvety epidermis. North Sea, Atlantic, Mediterranean. Fairly common.

152 **Cut Trough Shell,** *Spisula (Mactra) subtruncata.* Small, triangular species, 25 mm long; milk white. North Sea, Atlantic, Mediterranean. Fairly common.

153 **Thick Trough Shell,** *Spisula solida* L. Thick, 25-40 mm long; very prominent growth lines. North Sea, Atlantic. Very common.

150 a
150 b
149
152
151
153

154 **Common Otter Shell,** *Lutraria elliptica* Lamk. Edible. Shells 50-150 mm long, oblong in shape; white and pink, with brown periostracum. North Sea, Mediterranean. Rather rare.

155 **Oblong Otter Shell,** *Lutraria oblonga (magna).* Edible. Differs from No. 154 in its more definitely oblong shape; rounded posteriorly. North Sea, Mediterranean. Rather rare.

Gapers and **Basket Shells,** *Myidae.* Adductor muscle scars equal; pallial sinus; as in the trough shells, the ligament is internal in a special pit or chondrophore. However, the chondrophore is formed more distinctly and grips the interior of the shell like a spur.

156 **Sand Gaper** or **Soft-shelled Clam,** *Mya arenaria* L. Edible. Very similar to *Lutraria elliptica* in shape, but with a spur for the ligament projecting prominently from the hinge; 50-150 mm long. North Sea, Atlantic. Fairly common.

157 **Blunt Gaper,** *Mya truncata* L. Very much more obtuse than No. 156. North Sea, Atlantic. Fairly common.

154
155
156
157

158 **Common Basket Shell,** *Corbula gibba* Olivi. Small shell, 4-12 mm long, with unequal valves (the larger right valve extending beyond the left one). Lives in rocks, in holes excavated by boring molluscs. North Sea, Atlantic, Mediterranean. Fairly common.

Rock Borers, *Saxicavidae.* Bivalves living in rocks; external ligament; teeth below the beak very small or completely absent.

159 **Rock Borer,** *Saxicava rugosa* L. Beak close to posterior margin; slightly inequivalve; 26 mm long; hinge lacks teeth. Lives inside stones. North Sea, Atlantic, Mediterranean. Rather rare.

Scrobiculariids, *Scrobiculariidae.* Adductor muscle scars equal; pallial sinus; ligament internal in an oval chondrophore.

160 **Peppery Furrow Shell,** *Scrobicularia piperata* Poiret. Edible. Flat, round shell, 30-40 mm in diameter. North Sea, Atlantic, Mediterranean, in estuaries. Common.

161 *Syndosmya alba.* Small, white, polished shell; 17 mm long. North Sea, Atlantic, Mediterranean. Fairly common.

Thraciids, *Thraciidae.* Inequivalve, brittle; ligament internal on a cartilage.

162 *Thracia papyracea.* Thin, 30 mm long; protruding crest running from the beak to the rear; white, matt. North Sea, Atlantic, Mediterranean. Fairly common.

Pandora's Boxes, *Pandoridae.* As in thraciids.

163 **Pandora Shell,** *Pandora inaequivalvis (albida).* Valves very unequal, the right one flat, the left one convex; mother-of-pearl interior. North Sea, Atlantic, Mediterranean. Common.

158
159
160
161
163
162

Razor Shells, *Solenidae.* Adductor muscle scars unequal; pallial sinus; oblong; hollow canal at the end of the shell.

164 **Sword Razor,** *Ensis ensis.* Edible. Slightly curved, 80-200 mm long; one valve has 1 tooth, the other has 2. North Sea, Atlantic, Mediterranean. Common.

165 **Pod Razor,** *Ensis siliqua* L. Edible. As in No. 164, has 1 tooth on one valve, 2 teeth on the other, somewhat smaller valve; straight shell. Rather rare in the Atlantic, common in the Mediterranean.

166 **Grooved Razor,** *Solen marginatus* Penn. Edible. Differs from Nos. 164 and 165 in having only 1 tooth on each valve. Atlantic. Very common.

167 *Solecurtus strigillatus.* Large, 40-60 mm long; shorter than the three species above; two white rays on a pink background. Mediterranean. Common.

168 *Zozia antiquata.* Smaller than No. 167; coloured white, with a thin, greenish periostracum. Atlantic, Mediterranean. Rather rare.

169 **Pod Shell,** *Pharus legumen.* Oblong like the grooved razor, but rounded at both ends. White and pink, often with a shiny, yellowish epidermis; 40-100 mm long. North Sea, Atlantic, Mediterranean. Rather rare.

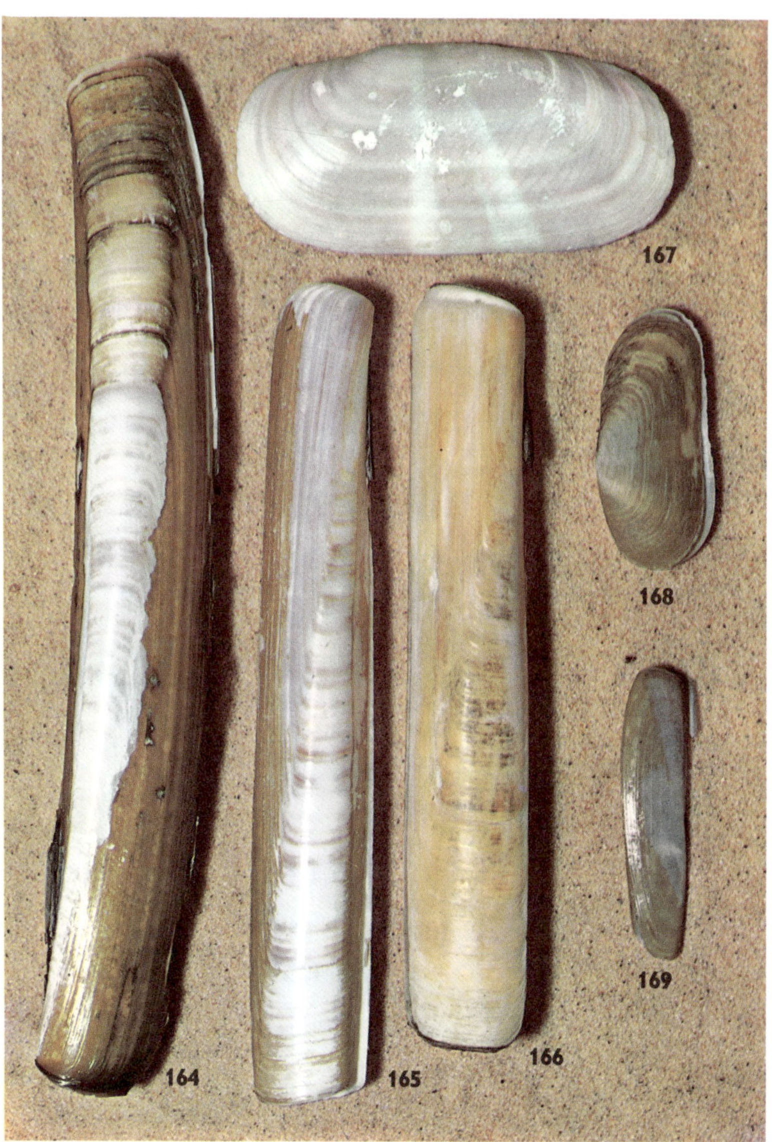

167
168
169
164
165
166

Piddocks, *Pholadidae.* Adductor muscle scars unequal; pallial sinus. The species of this family bore into rocks. Valves gape at front and back; no hinge; no ligament.

170 **Common Piddock,** *Pholas dactylus* L. Edible. About 100 mm in size; near the beak there are 2 pairs of accessory plates for the protection of the valves. Lives in rocks. Atlantic, Mediterranean. Common.

171 **White Piddock,** *Barnea candida* L. Both valves covered with spines; 40-70 mm long; only 1 protoplax present on the dorsal side. North Sea, Atlantic, Mediterranean. Fairly common.

Flask Shells, *Gastrochaenidae.* Very closely related to the piddocks. The species of this family also live in rocks, but the shells have a ligament.

172 **Flask Shell,** *Gastrochaena dubia* Penn. Small, 10-20 mm, very brittle; wide anterior gape. North Sea, Atlantic, Mediterranean. Fairly common.

Shipworms, *Teredinidae.* The species of this family bore into wood; small, brittle shells, covering only the extreme end of the animal's body; the rest of the body is surrounded by a long, calcareous tube.

173 **Shipworm,** *Teredo norvegica* Spgl. The illustration shows part of the calcareous tube. The valves themselves are very fragile and very difficult to obtain. Bore deep, chalk-lined burrows up to 300 mm long in wooden boats, posts, etc. North Sea, Atlantic, Mediterranean. Common.

Fan Mussels, *Pinnidae.* Adductor muscle scars unequal; valves are mother-of-pearl inside, sometimes have ears in the region of the hinge, are sometimes long and triangular; flat, slightly inequivalve shells.

174 **Pough Pen Shell,** *Pinna nobilis.* Large, 150-600 mm long, triangular shell with wavy growth lines; covered with overlapping scales. Mediterranean. Rather rare. Smaller variation in the Mediterranean and Atlantic: Pinna pectinata L., lacking the scaly covering.

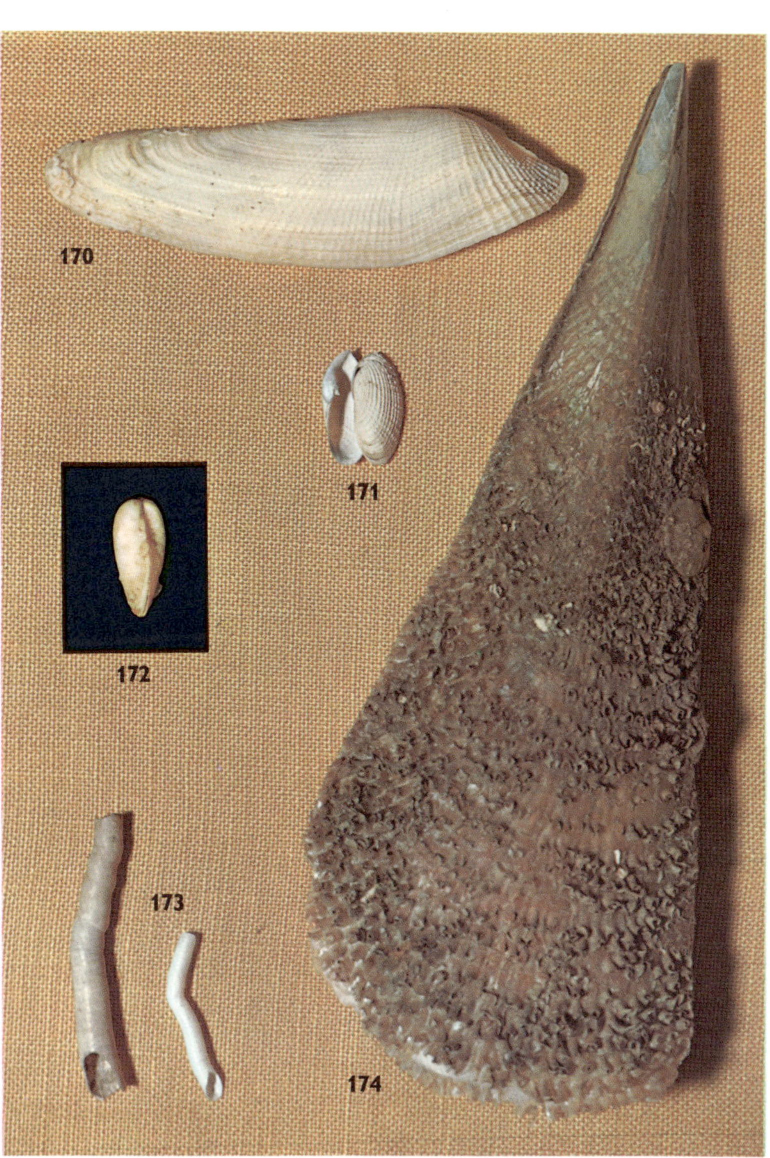
170
171
172
173
174

Wing Oysters, *Pteriidae.* As in fan mussels.

175 **Wing Oyster,** *Pteria hirundo* L. Attractive shells, mother-of-pearl interior; violet reflexions on the outer surface. Size of shell 30-90 mm. Mediterranean. Common.

Mussels, *Mytilidae.* Adductor muscle scars unequal; valves equal, swollen, mother-of-pearl inside.

176 **Common Mussel,** *Mytilus edulis* L. Blue-black; mother-of-pearl only slightly shiny. Atlantic, Mediterranean. Very common. Cultivated as a delicacy.

177 **Mediterranean Mussel,** *Mytilus galloprovincialis* Lam. Edible. Broader than No. 176 in the beak area. Mediterranean. Common.

178 *Mytilaster minimus.* Interesting because of its small size. Atlantic. Common.

179 **Bearded Horse Mussel,** *Modiolus barbatus* L. Similar to Nos. 176-8, but rather trapezoid, beak not at end of shell; 30-80 mm, covered with more or less long fringes. Atlantic, Mediterranean. Fairly common.

180 **Tulip Mussel,** *Modiolus adriaticus.* Smaller than No. 179, without fringes. North Sea, Atlantic, Mediterranean. Fairly common.

181 **Marbled Crenella,** *Musculus marmoratus (modiolaria marmorata, crenella marmorata).* Small, 10-15 mm; green, mottled. Lives in the mantle of ascidians. Atlantic, Mediterranean. Rather rare.

182 **Date Mussel,** *Lithophaga lithophaga.* Cylindrical shell, 20-60 mm in size, swollen at the front; yellow and brown. Lives between stones. Mediterranean. Fairly common.

175
180
176
181
178
179
182
177

Scallops, *Pectinidae.* Only one adductor muscle. Not mother-of-pearl; regular shape; radiating ribs.

183a **Great Scallop,** *Pecten maximus* L. Edible. Large shell, with unequal valves, the right one convex, the left one flat; regular, rounded, radiating folds; grooves striated; 80-150 mm. North Sea, Atlantic. Common.

183b Pecten is represented in the Mediterranean by the **St. James' Shell,** *Pecten Jacobaeus* L. Edible. It too has radiating ribs, but they are angular; grooves not striated.

184 **Queen Scallop,** *Chlamys opercularis* L. Edible. 10 mm in size; both valves convex, but unequal. Various colours. Atlantic, Mediterranean. Common.

185 *Chlamys glabra.* Edible. Very similar to No. 184, but smaller; brown stripes. Mediterranean. Common.

186 **Variegated Scallop,** *Chlamys varia* L. Edible. Both valves convex, with numerous, radiating, very thin folds; ears of the shells unequal; colour variable; 40-60 mm. North Sea, Atlantic, Mediterranean. Common.

187 *Chlamys multistriata.* Small shell, 20-30 mm; numerous radiating ribs. Adheres to rocks or shells. Mediterranean. Fairly common.

184
185
183 a
186
187
183 b

Spondylids, *Spondylidae.* Only one adductor muscle scar; very inequivalve; radiating folds with spines.

188 *Spondylus gaederopus.* 50-80 mm, strong, spiny ribs. Adheres to rocks. Mediterranean. Fairly common.

File shells, *Limidae.* Only one adductor muscle scar; equivalve; ears only slightly developed.

189 **Spiny Lima Clam,** *Lima lima.* Size of shell 25-35 mm; radiating ribs with laminated tubercles. Mediterranean. Rather rare.

190 **Gaping File Shell,** *Lima hians* Gm. Very brittle, only 10-15 mm; lives on rocks. Atlantic, Mediterranean. Rather rare.

Oysters, *Ostreidae.* Only one adductor muscle scar; unequal valves are irregular in shape.

191 **Flat** or **Native Oyster,** *Ostrea edulis* L. Round, only slightly convex; lives on the sea bottom, forming oyster beds. North Sea, Atlantic, Mediterranean. (Also cultivated in artificially created oyster beds.)

192 **Portuguese Oyster,** *Gryphaea angulata* L. Edible. Differs from No. 191 in its more oval shell and the pronounced trough-like form of the left (lower) valve. Introduced from Portugal, where it occurs naturally in the Tejo (Tagus) estuary. Cultivated on oyster farms.

Saddle Oysters or **Jingle Shells,** *Anomiidae.* Only one adductor muscle scar; thin shells; adhere to other shells.

193 **Saddle Oyster** or **Jingle Shell,** *Anomia ephippium* Lamk. Edible. The lower (right) valve follows the shape of the base to which the mollusc adheres; muscles are attached to the base through a hole in the lower valve. North Sea, Atlantic, Mediterranean. Very common.

188
190
189
193
192
191

INDEX

of the common names of the snails and bivalve shells described. Names marked with an asterisk* are only described, not illustrated. Figures denote the continuous numbering of the examples.

Families